forest faith

Richard Dahlstrom

FINDING HOPE AND WHOLENESS
BY LEARNING TO PRAY AMONG THE TREES

Practices by Abby Odio & Illustrations by Abigail Platter

Forest Faith:
Finding Hope and Wholeness By Learning to Pray Among the Trees

Richard Dahlstrom

Illustrations by Abigail Platter

Practices by Abby Odio

Copyright © 2021 Bethany. Community Church

churchbcc.org

All rights reserved.

Covid shut the world down, and for me that meant staying home in the forest. The isolation began with 10 feet of snow on the ground, and continued through two melting springs, two summers, a fall, and a full winter. It was there in isolation that I began paying attention to the trees. They'd always been there, but I'm not sure I'd ever paid attention as I was too busy passing through, on my way here or there. Once I started looking, I started learning, and once I started learning, I started giving thanks to God for the wisdom of the trees, and all they have to teach me.

This book, then, is dedicated to the Creator who initiates and sustains all life,
To the trees, who receive and give and serve us all so generously, and without fanfare,
And to Donna who for over forty years, has taught me to pay attention to what God says through creation
Thank You

Needed: A New Way of Seeing

I pray that the eyes of your heart may be opened in order that you may know the hope to which God has called you. ~Paul the Apostle

The world we see with our senses is very different than the world we see through our essence. Our senses perceive the world of appearance. Our essence perceives the deeper layers of existence. ~Peter Kabakci

They have eyes, but they do not see. ~Jesus the Christ

* * *

Cinderella goes to the ball, falls in love, and escapes oppression. The Beast escapes the prison of his cursed body by learning to love. The farm boy overcomes obstacles and finds true love with the princess.

Most people love tales of transformation and movement. Oppression to freedom, loneliness to love, sickness to health, war to peace, poverty to abundance; these are just a few of the plot lines that captivate, motivate, and inspire us. The genres in which most of these stories are categorized are "fairy tales" and "fiction." Though these stories warm hearts, our fundamental paradigm is that they offer us a pleasant escape from reality. We'll spend an hour or two captivated by triumphs of grace, vulnerability, justice, courage, and of course, "true love." But then it's back to the real world of suffering, competition, and for many, profound feelings of inadequacy. To quote the protagonist named Wesley, the farm boy in The Princess Bride, "Life *is* pain, highness. Anyone who says otherwise is selling something."

Of course. Simply perusing your news feed on any given day will expose multiple shootings, a government somewhere on the brink of toppling, the absolute frustration of political paralysis and corruption, racism, poverty, increasingly frequent "once in a thousand years" weather events, and refugees risking their lives by fleeing because they know staying means certain death. Pay too much attention, and you'll find yourself either spiraling into depression, fortifying yourself for battle, or buying into one of the million escape mechanisms for sale. This, it appears, is the way of it.

Something I call the "domination model" is at play in most of this bad news we digest. It's a value system that saturates most cultures and political structures, along with many family systems. This model says that the point of the game is to gain more: whether its money, or power, or influence, or market share, the domination model motivates people to climb. This model is behind slavery and colonialism ("we need more land and resources"), it's behind most 20th century wars (which were fought around the subject of who would control certain geographical spaces). The reason it's called a domination model is because the whole system is predicated on having winners and losers. I gain more land by taking. I gain more power by enslaving, oppressing, using.

The domination model doesn't just include people dominating people. It also includes the human world dominating the rest of creation. When you over-harvest and over-fish, or when you clear cut the forest without regard for its long term health, there is usually an immediate bump in profits. When that bump in profits drives decision making, it's easy to see why the domination model is so deeply embedded. Why throw a fish back when you can sell it? Why run a small organic farm when, for the same amount of work, you can run an industrial farm and make more money? The immediate profit - not the air, or ocean, or water table, or trees, or endangered species - becomes the primary, perhaps even the sole, consideration. We're rich all right, at least we who are at the top. But it's unsustainable, and unjust[1].

We know, many of us, that the system is deeply broken. Yet it seems there's no way to fix it. As Bruce Hornsby sings, "that's just the way it is - some thing will never change..." Buying and selling, dominating and enslaving, harvesting until there's nothing left - that's the way of it.

Or is it? Let's presume for a moment that our Creator has

---

[1] Hosea 4:1-3 speaks of a time when "cursing, lying, stealing, murder, and bloodshed are rampant", and says that as a result, "the land mourns." The domination model destroys both human dignity and the earth's beauty and sustainability.

put "eternity in our hearts" as the wise man said in the book of Ecclesiastes[2]. What if our delight in fairy tales exists because these stories point to a deeper, truer, more lasting reality? What if present reality, called "this world" in the Bible, is indeed passing away? What if the domination model is on the way out, eventually to be evicted from the universe by the spirit of Christ? What if, when the end of the story is known and experienced, all this suffering will be seen as a passing chapter, an afternoon storm in a universe shot through with glory, beauty, intimacy, and hope? What if the *real* world, the *eternal* world, is more like the fairy tale than the news feed?

The stunning and radical message from God is that there's a world where every tear is dried from every eye, every disease healed, all wars ended, justice and reconciliation brought to life, celebration, and beauty, and love all flourishing. It has at least two different names in the Bible. Its called *Shalom* in the Old Testament, which is a Hebrew word that is best described as perfect flourishing for every element of creation. Later, Jesus will expand on this concept and call it the "Kingdom of God." He too paints pictures of justice and generosity, healing and abundance, and brings a special focus to the inclusive nature of the kingdom by welcoming, affirming, and even exalting people who conventional thinkers of the day would have deemed as unworthy outcasts and in some cases even executed.

After Jesus, Paul the Apostle will expand on this shalom/kingdom theme in many ways through his writings. One of the most poignant articulations is found in his letter to the church at Ephesus, where he says history is headed toward

---

[2] Ecclesiastes 3:10 indicates that every human has deep longings for the "better world" of eternity, which is a world of justice, beauty, healing, hope, mercy, abundance, and peace.

"the summing up of all things in Christ, things in heaven and things on the earth[3]." This radical declaration says that when our current era ends, every atom in the universe will be saturated with the glory of Christ, which means that justice, peace, beauty, intimacy, joy, abundance, health, and hope will be the new normal - and not just for some, but for, as the text says, "all things." If this is where history is headed, it changes everything, including a fundamental overall shift in how we view the world. Hope begins to displace despair. Even though we still grieve over the realities of living in a broken time and place, at a deeper level we have a quiet confidence in the trajectory of the universe, a confidence that Shalom of Christ wins!

It gets better though. This eventual reality of perfection isn't wholly future. It is, in some measure at least, here now. Jesus said it this way: "The kingdom of God is among you[4]," which can be translated with equal legitimacy "within you." You might be Cinderella, but you're also a queen. You might be a farm boy, but soon you'll marry the princess. Jesus and Paul both tell us there are two realities: there's a world of suffering, injustice, and oppression that is with us because the domination model is here now, a passing storm on the way to eternity. It's capable of clouding our vision so thoroughly that we begin to believe it is our deepest and most abiding reality, which then leads us to fight back and live stress-induced lives, or drop out in despair. Either way, we miss an invitation to experience the Shalom of God's good reign as our primary default reality, which is intended to be our truest and deepest life.

It is precisely in these two competing views of reality that the battle of our daily lives is fought. If the domination model

---

[3] Ephesians 1:1–12
[4] Luke 17:21

is our deepest reality, we adapt to its values of conquest, struggle, individualism and its ugly counterpart, tribalism. It makes sense that we'd come to see this as the default reality because most of what we absorb each day shouts it to be true, real, lasting. As a result we legitimize the struggle and try to build our lives. If we succeed, we work to guard what we've gained from the world of predators out there. Along the way we experience sporadic escapes. Sometimes there are genuine moments of Shalom, like when we experience true intimacy, generosity, reconciliation, justice, and hospitality. Other times we use toxic escape mechanisms to avoid the dulling pain of living in this dark world of battles. Indulge often enough in the same escape, and you'll wire your brain to demand it over and over again, in bigger doses. That's called addiction, or idolatry, depending on your worldview.

Jesus landed on this planet in the midst of an oppressive empire with the domination model on full display. It was a world filled with haves and have-nots, of people lording it over others, where the empire and its values were the only normal available. Jesus then speaks into this prevailing paradigm of struggle and suggests we learn to live more like flowers and birds than empire soldiers. He sleeps in the bottom of a boat in the midst of a life threatening storm. He touches the untouchables, crosses social divides with ease and delight, forgives his tormenters, and unleashes scathing rebukes on the institutional religious professionals of his day. What reality is he living in?

He's living in Shalom, in God's kingdom reality. Jesus says that beneath the veil of the domination model, there's deeper, abiding rule governing the universe. You see it in intact ecosystems, which is why he points to wildflowers as an illustration. It's declared in the "peace with God" that is a reality through Christ. It's seen in Paul's remarkable declaration that, in spite of the current existence of multiple dividing walls among class, gender, and race, there is "no longer Jew nor Greek, slave nor free, male nor female." He says dividing walls have already been broken down. When Christ declared "it is finished" on the cross, the eternal reality of God's good reign over the universe began its healing work.

Of course, as the author of the letter to the Hebrews says, "we don't yet see all things subject to him[5]." The fading veil of darkness and death remains, and a list of its ugly fruits would extend for pages. What makes the gospel remarkably liberating good news, though, is the declaration that there's a different, more foundational, reality (what C.S. Lewis called the "deep magic" in the Chronicles of Narnia), and it's both God's desire and design that we live out from this. When we do, we'll be able to peel back the fading veil of domination and reveal God's good reign in our bodies, our communities, and our families. It begins by gaining the capacity to see and believe that there *is* a just, beautiful, substantially healed world right here, right now. It's visible in the seasons, the sunrises, the unanticipated moments of intimacy, and countless acts of service, courage, and generosity. It's in your creativity, your confessions, and your giving and receiving of grace. God's good reign is, when you have eyes to see, truly all around us and within us.

Gaining the capacity to see that reality and live out from it is what this little book is all about. We'll gain that capacity by meditating on the truth that God's glory is ever present - above us, beneath us, around us, and within us. We'll go deeper into each of these four declarations, continuing to meditate on them so that the truth God has declared will increasingly become the lens through which we see all of life. The results have been transformative and liberating at every level of my life. I write in hopes that you too can join me in

---

[5] Hebrews 2:8

this journey of learning to see the world as saturated with Christ.

Why meditation?

Meditation actually runs deep through the history of God's people[6] so wisdom declares we need to pull it off the shelf and rediscover it for our 21st century lives. Here's what we'll learn:

To *meditate* simply means to chew on something over and over again, as articulated in Psalm 1 and Joshua 1. We all do it when we sing the lyrics of a song that gets stuck in our head, or talk to ourselves, repeating the lie we're worthless because of a bad decision we made, or that we're amazing because of that promotion we got. In this sense, we all meditate already. Our goal is to do an intervention so that, as the psalmist prays in Psalm 19, the meditations of our hearts become acceptable to God. Don't misread that to believe that God is sitting somewhere really angry with us until our meditations are acceptable. But, rather, God's desire is that our meditations align with truth and reality, because God wants *our lives to align with truth and reality!* The results of such alignment is that we're healed and empowered, enabled to play our part in unveiling God's good reign in our world. Jesus' language for this is his promise that we'll become "rivers of living water," better able to bless and serve a parched world.

God knows our world is thirsty. Most of us, in our moments of honesty, are able to acknowledge that we ourselves are thirsty too. Many are quick to admit that for all our Bible studies, church attendance, other forms of spiritual practices, and doctrinal or political debates, our souls are still

---

[6] Joshua 1, Psalm 1, Psalm 19:15, Psalm 104:34

parched. We don't need more information. We need the living water that is Christ to flow freely *into us* and *through us*.

What you hold in your hands is a simple guide to help you develop a genuinely Christ-filled practice of meditation. The phrase "Christ-filled" is chosen carefully, because meditation practice here guides you to focus on what I believe to be the most important and life-changing truth in the universe, which is that the Spirit of our Creator has saturated every atom of the entire universe with the Creator's life. Every branch of every tree; the creatures in the deepest parts of the sea and the highest birds in the sky; the soil, streams and rivers; the trees and shrubs; the mushrooms and bears; and yes, even you and me!

Let it sink into the depth of our being that all the political posturing, all the righteous indignation spewed on our 24/7 news cycle, all the storming of castles, all the disease and isolation is, while its own form of reality, nothing more than a temporary veil. If Jesus is right, the kingdoms of this world are passing away, and when that happens all that remains will be that which is shot through and saturated with our Creator's love, beauty, and glory.

Imagine becoming deeply rooted in the reality that the glory of Christ is everywhere. Imagine if that reality was governing your daily state of being and responses, rather than the news, or social media visions of other people's fulfillment. This is why the psalmist wrote that those who mediate on God's revelation consistently will be a constant source of life, like a tree planted by a stream. Continually drawing upon the streams of life-giving reality, such a person *will be fruitful,* as the vibrancy of divine life will flow through them.

The Bowl is Not the Ingredient

The last thing that must be said before starting our journey is that "meditation" per se isn't some secret sauce. It might be true that paying attention to one's breath and slowing down a racing mind has some health benefits; but that's hardly the main thing. The real goal isn't meditating; it's reconnection with our Creator so that we can live the life for which we've been created. Then we can serve our world and help awaken the spirits of others stuck in the many forms of blindness brought on by the lies of our world. Such lies lead to excesses of anxiety, shame, fear, drink, careless sex, loneliness, greed, and competition, to name a few. The fruit of believing lies is all around us, both inside and outside communities of faith.

Remember Jesus' words: there's an enemy whose goal is 'steal, kill, and destroy[7]'. The enemy is called "the liar." Our best lives are stolen from us to the extent that we believe the lies and illusions of our world. These lies present themselves through our culture, passing judgements, appetites, and moods, and to the extent we treat them as real and true, they determine our priorities and responses. Jesus said that the better way, the path of freedom is to "know the truth," but to know it Jesus said we need to abide in Jesus' word. The one who abides is the one who remains, and thus becomes deeply connected to two realities, 1) that the whole world is saturated with Christ, and 2) that you yourself have Christ living in you. What better way to abide in these truths than to meditate on them daily?

The prayer we'll be using has evolved from what is called St. Patrick's "Encircling Prayer," which we'll look at in the next chapter. We'll be praying and meditating on four truths, each of which call for a response or declaration from us:

---

[7] John 10:10

* * *

> Christ above me. I receive.
> Christ beneath me. I am rooted.
> Christ around me. I am connected.
> Christ within me. I am called.

You're encouraged to use all four declarations as your meditation from the start, but focus your study on one of these each week for four weeks, engaging in the suggested practices along the way. The results will be a spirit awakened to the deeper, eternal realities of the Creator's perpetual presence as gift-giver and sustainer of life. This eternal reality, though always true, is too often choked out by what Jesus calls "the cares of this world." It will be the different way of seeing that will slowly, over time, result in a different way of living. It's not a glamorous or loud path. Neither is it popular. Why would it be, when snake oil promising enlightenment via a weekend course, sleeping elixir, or online conference hits our inboxes weekly, even daily for some? Jesus does not offer quick fixes. Maybe this is why Jesus calls his road the narrow one. Those who follow it aren't busy making noise, and may never make headlines either. They're just quietly showing up to reality and day by day, so slowly as to be imperceptible, becoming more like Jesus.

Are you ready? Let the journey begin.

The Encircling Prayer

Our God is the God of all, God of heaven and earth, sea and river. He inspires all things; He quickens all things. He kindles the light of the sun and of the moon. ~St. Patrick

*Earth is crammed with heaven,
and every common bush afire with God:
But only he who sees takes off his shoes - Elizabeth Barrett Browning*

The History of St. Patrick's Breastplate Prayer
Our encircling meditation has its roots in the prayer for protection offered by St. Patrick, likely in 433 CE. The Celts had an ancient template to guide people in their prayers for

protection. It was called a *lorica* or *breastplate prayer*. When Patrick came to faith in Christ, he was intent on lighting a fire on the hill of Slane in celebration of Easter. His intent was to do so as a means of declaring Christ as the eternal light which will never be quenched, the greater and deeper reality that transcends all human kingdoms. Patrick knew that the light from his fire would be visible in Tara where the high king Laeghaire resided. The high-king, though, was intent on lighting his own fire that night and had given a decree that no other fires be lit, in order that it would be clear to all that the high-king was *the* source of light, warmth, and provision.

In a world of warring domination systems, high-kings are threatened by strange fires. Laeghaire's wizards warned that if Patrick's fire wasn't quenched, it would consume all other fires and light the land until the end of time. His fire was received as a supreme threat, much like the story of King Herod's hatred of Jesus, or any contemporary ruler's fear of any voice other than their own! Rather than extinguishing his fire, though, Patrick prayed what has come to be know as the Hymn of St. Patrick.

Embedded in this prayer is a stanza declaring the presence of Christ in our world to be a total reality:

Christ beside me, Christ before me;
Christ behind me, Christ within me;
Christ beneath me, Christ above me;
Christ to the right of me, Christ to the left of me;
Christ in my lying, my sitting, my rising;
Christ in the heart of all who know me,
Christ on the tongue of all who meets me
Christ in the eye of all who see me
Christ in the ear of all who hear me

Patrick is praying that the reality of Christ as the ever-present source of life, beauty, abundance, peace, justice, joy, hope, and blessing would rise to the surface and become his experienced earthly reality, not just a mystical, heavenly dream. One ancient mystic called this "the divine music which is always coursing through the universe" and while it might be a stretch to some literalists to call it that, ponder this: Jesus said that if people fail to praise him, the rocks would cry out. The Psalms are filled with language about creation praising the Creator. Job 38 says that "the morning stars sang together at the outset of creation", and Psalm 148 paints the picture in which a veritable symphony of creation is praising the Lord: fruit trees and cedars, mountains and valleys, sea creatures and birds, wild animals and cattle, fire and hail, snow and mist. It's a poetic way of saying that all creation is made to be shot through with glory, the end of which will be to offer a constant flood of gifts to the world as offerings of praise. That's the eternal music that's always humming above, below, around, and within us.

The world is also fallen. As a result, the eternal music of praise is often drowned out by deafening tones of conflict, work stress, afflictions, time pressures, family demands, relationship challenges, and more. Each of these creates its own dissonance, its own volume. Sometimes these challenges create a deafening decibel level, drowning out the chords of deeper reality. The noise affects our spirits as we lose sight of our truest identity and calling. It affects our souls, because without a solid spirit foundation, our ego is all we have. In our attempts to defend it, we become petty, defensive, angry, insecure, and cynical. These internal problems eventually present in our bodies too, as stress hormones pulsing through the body, elevated heart rate and blood pressure, sleep problems, or just the simple desire to drown oneself in ice cream.

When our misalignment with reality becomes chronic, it

creates feelings of frustration and burnout, leading to mean-spirited responses to people, self-medicated escape plans, and a dozen other toxicities, each drawing down our reserves even more, until eventually we can't continue in anything but the barest survival mode. Been there? Me too. A person can be filled with God language, church activities, and service projects without ever experiencing liberation from these problems!

The good news is that there's a way to turn down the volume on the steady diet of challenges we face. Meditating on the realities that transcend our day to day experiences enables us to navigate our world out from a place of wholeness. It requires we intentionally turn toward the deeper truths, the 'eternal music' as the Celts would call it, allowing them to literally overwhelm us, so that they become the lens through which we view the world.

It happened for Patrick. The high king sent soldiers to kill Patrick and extinguish the fire, but they failed on both goals, and the light of Christ literally began shining in Ireland that night. As a result, Patrick changed the course of Irish history and, some would say, all of western civilization.

As we focus on the fourfold "saturation prayer," we too will come to discover that the light of Christ is always shining. In the darkest moments of history, both personal and cultural, countless Christ followers have shone with a brightness inexplicable in human terms. A study of their lives reveals that they'd found the capacity to live out from a different reality than the prevailing narratives of our world. They were, indeed, saturated with Christ.

Before others began demonstrating this power, Jesus cleared the way with a remarkable demonstration of how the higher world and this present world are related. The story begins on a dark and stormy night.

* * *

Ground Zero: Christ Saturation

At the end of a full day, Jesus' disciples were out on a lake, in a boat with him. It was an evening outing, or maybe an overnight trip. After they'd set out, a strong wind kicked up, strong enough that the disciples feared for their lives. Meanwhile, Jesus is asleep "inside the boat" we're told. We're given enough detail to know he had "his head on a pillow." The followers of Jesus woke him up and said, "Teacher, don't you care that we're perishing?" They were overwhelmed by circumstances beyond their control, afraid. In their minds, their lives were at risk. Jesus, though, was sleeping soundly through it all. They wake him, and he speaks a word or two to the storm. It stops. He then says, "Why are you afraid? Do you still have no faith?" and then, we presume, immediately goes back to sleep[8].

The story illustrates two different ways of navigating the storms of the life. For Jesus' followers, the circumstances take on the character of ominous threat, beyond their capacity to control it. They didn't create the storm; it's happening *to* them, in just the same way a pandemic, cancer, downsizing, market crashes, broken arms, aging parents, challenging children, car accidents, forest fires, bike accidents, betrayal, hurricanes, avalanches, and much of the rest that is terrible in life, happens to us. "Acts of God," we're told, aren't covered by insurance because actuaries have zero chance of predicting them. For a decent slice of life, this is the way of it. We're almost bystanders as things appear to unravel. It creates a fight or flight response in us, but neither are actually doable, so instead, our whole being gets stuck in stress mode, afflicting both soul and body. Some lose sleep. Others eat too much. Others stop eating. Others drink. Blood pressure rises. Intimacy falls. Peace moves away. It's somewhere still, we

---

[8] Mark 4:35-41

suppose, just no longer at our house. It's a terrible place to be.

Meanwhile, Jesus, asleep in the boat, exemplifies a different paradigm. He's in the same storm, subject to the same waves. He sleeps though, instead of fretting. Its not because he has divine powers at his disposal. If that were the case, he would have praised them for coming and asking the Lord of the universe to pull off a miracle, the same way he praised the Royal official who sought Jesus out to heal his son. Instead he rebukes them, and asks if they "still have no faith?" What's he saying?

He's saying that despite the fact that it's a fallen world filled with storms, it's also true that there's an unshakable goodness and peace coursing through the universe. It's a sort of bedrock confidence that, in spite of the current cultural, national, global and personal messes we navigate, God is still good, still there, still the ultimate source of all that is just, right, and beautiful. The rains still fall, watering the earth. Trees still exhale oxygen so that we can inhale another breath. There are seasons bringing the bursting forth of life, playfulness, intimacy. There are also moments when we're given a taste of our eternal longings for justice, beauty, and peace. All these bear witness to a different, and - God would say - more abiding reality.

People of faith believe that this is because the cross and resurrection set in motion a "making new of all things[9]." Storms will happen, no doubt. They'll hit us personally at various times in our lives, and surely we'll learn of storms in other lives and cultures every single day. Storms pass though. The abiding reality is different, better, Shalom. Between the present storehouses of outlandish beauty and provision, and the assurance of a glorious future, we too can sleep in the

---

[9] Isaiah 65:17 is just one of several places where the "all things new" language appears in the Bible

boat. Look at what one Psalm writer declares:

> *God is our refuge and strength*
> *A very present help in trouble.*
> *Therefore we will not fear, through the earth should change*
> *And through the mountains slip into the heart of the sea;*
> *Though its waters roar and foam*
> *Though the mountains quake at its swelling pride*
> *There is a river whose streams make glad the city of God,*
> *The holy dwelling place of the Most High*
> *God is the midst of her, she will not be moved*[10]...

There's the fleeting reality that our world is broken. There's a primary, more permanent, and hence more substantial reality that our world is shot through with the glory of God. St. Patrick's prayer was that the permanent reality would prevail in his experience, that he would see Christ surrounding him in the midst of his trials and battles, going before him, remaining behind him, abiding within him, and supporting him from below.

In God's wisdom, God has left us revelations to declare to us that we can confidently claim this reality, because God has declared that, indeed, Christ is above us, beneath us, around us, and within us, as we shall see in the chapters ahead. To the extent that we believe this to be true, our eyes begin to open, and we see this presence in our daily experiences. This leads to what Isaiah declares:

> *In returning and rest you shall be saved*
> *In quietness and trust shall be your strength*[11]

When we tap into this greater and more enduring reality, we

---

[10] Psalm 46

[11] Isaiah 30:15

find rest, quietness, trust, and strength. That's the good news. Unfortunately, Isaiah continues with one more line:

But you were unwilling

Ugh. Our unwillingness is at the root of all our striving, our wars, our angry mobs, our sleepless nights of regret and fearful anticipation. Unwilling to rest in the greater and enduring reality that the world, despite all its pain and suffering, is shot through with the glory of Christ. Jesus tells a story in which our capacity to live fruitful and meaningful lives is contingent on whether or not we allow this primary reality of God's goodness and control to govern our lives or not. In his story our lives are like soil, and the goodness of God is the seed planted in the soil. It's a good seed, made for love, creativity, service, generosity, joy, and peace. It's vital to remind ourselves that God's desire, God's invitation, and God's provision are all made with a view toward wholeness, healing, life! The challenge? Unless the soil receives proper care, either suffering, wealth, or the pursuit of wealth, will become the dominant narrative, and then the seed won't produce. Good soil is needed.

This is why meditation on the primary reality that the "earth is the Lord's and the fulness within it" is so vital for our own spirit, soul, and body health. In this booklet we'll meditate on four realities, and to the extent that our whole self - spirit, soul, and body - begins to align with these truths, we'll find ourselves increasingly reflecting the quiet confidence we long for, the confidence God wants us to enjoy. No matter what happens outwardly, the inner realities of Christ's power, beauty, generosity, justice, and compassion become our bedrock. They increasingly define us because, believing them to be true, we begin to see and know them in our experience. We don't wait to see before we believe. We believe in order that we might see. That's the life of faith; and people who practice it consistently have a decent shot at falling asleep in the boat, even in the storms.

Practice: Encircling Meditation

Please don't get tripped up on the word meditation. It's a concept that comes right out of the Bible, as you can discover in many places. The original word has connotations similar to that of a cow chewing its food over and over again, which is a way of saying that the more you allow your mind to dwell on some reality, the more that reality begins to define you. Elsewhere in the Bible that principle is articulated this way: "As a person thinks in his/her heart, so is he/she." Think about your failures all the time and you'll end up feeling like a failure. Think about your sexual desires all the time and you'll become defined by your lust for sex. Think about your bank account all the time and your money will define you.

Think about what God has declared regarding the reality of God's redeeming presence in the whole universe, and in you, and slowly, over time, you'll begin to be defined by that glorious and liberating truth. As that reality begins to change your perceptions, you yourself begin to change. You move away from anxiety, toward peace. Away from shame, toward self-acceptance and the capacity to live by grace. I could go on, but you get the idea. The transformation rarely happens in our lives when we simply say to ourselves, "This week I'll work on being patient, or generous, or joyful," and then set off to change ourselves. This doesn't work because we're not designed to change ourselves; we're designed to awaken and respond to our invitation to union with our Creator, and it's our Creator who changes us.

The transformation happens as the lies that fill our minds, emotions, and bodies are exposed and replaced by divine truths. The process is more like trees growing than the creation of a meal. It's slow, mostly imperceptible, "from glory to glory" as Paul the Apostle says. Yet, it's happening, even when we're not aware of it! This process allows our truest nature, which has been functionally dead by virtue of being buried under layers of cultural and spiritual rubbish, to wake up, transformed by Christ, and take control of every fiber of our being. When that happens, Christ's resurrection life begins to pour through us in more ways than we'd have anticipated. The result becomes a reorienting of our lives so that our remaining chapters are characterized, not by perfection, but by ongoing transformation, with an increased capacity to bless and serve others in this broken, yet beautiful world.

A Primer for this Meditation:

It doesn't matter if you sit on a meditation pillow, walk slowly in a park, do dishes, or change beds. What's needed is simply enough mental space to focus, as much as possible, on four simple truths, and respond to each one. For your first times, though, it's maybe best if you sit, and essential that you hide your phone and other devices. There's nothing magical or legalistic about these recommendations; they just help you focus completely as you get a feel for it.

Once you're sitting, slow your breathing down and relax a bit. Once you've established a sense of presence and a rhythm of breathing, you'll say one of these declarations for each of four breaths:

Inhale One - "Christ Above Me"
   Exhale One - "I Receive"

Inhale Two - "Christ Beneath Me"
   Exhale Two - "I am Rooted"

***

Inhale Three - "Christ Around Me"
Exhale Three - "I'm Connected"

Inhale Four - "Christ Within Me"
Exhale Four - "I am Called"

Once you get the hang of this, set a timer for five minutes, and simply repeat these eternal truths slowly, again and again, seeking to be present with the meaning. You're *meditating* on the reality that God is in control of all things. God is raining down gifts every day. God is rooting your identity deeply in Christ so that you gain an increasing confidence and peace. God is connecting you with other people and the rest of creation, inviting you to a healthy giving and receiving. Finally, God is alive within you, as "Christ in you" becomes the hope of displaying glory in this world. You have a purpose, a calling!

In subsequent chapters, we'll unpack each of these realities, learning from the text of the Bible, and the text of creation as we see how the forest speaks of these things. Each truth will carry some practices with it as well. It's best to take your time with this, doing the the fourfold meditation on some sort of regular basis, but also going deep for a period with each declaration by doing the practices.

Why Meditation?

In a pragmatic, utilitarian, consumeristic age, there's no shortage of "self help" books, programs, seminars and online classes. Self-help though, is an oxymoron in my opinion, because what's needed is not a DIY strategy for changing *anything* about ourselves. What's actually needed is alignment with who our Creator has designed us to be, and that pursuit has no DIY path to discovery. Rather, it comes from receiving, believing, and responding to divine revelation. The truth is singing to us all the time through the sunrise and rain, the trees and vineyards, the fish and creatures, moments of intimacy, and groans of suffering. It's serenading us through God's text, from poetic creation stories in Genesis and Job, to the exodus of Jews. From Christ's words and actions and life and resurrection, to Paul's vision of radical union with God - the message is there: God is pouring God's life through the universe, through others made in God's image, and through (dare we believe it), our own lives! Let's live out from that reality more and more, starting today. Are you ready for the journey? Let's go!

Truth One: Christ Above Me - I Receive

*Every good and perfect gift is from above, coming down from the Father of heavenly light,
who does not change like shifting shadows.* ~James 1:17

The heavens are declaring the glory of God. ~Psalm 19

Learning from the Trees

I live in a forest east of Seattle. During the global pandemic the forest became my best theology teacher. When our just-shy-of-an-acre forest was clear-cut decades ago the loggers let three trees remain because, for various reasons, they didn't appear profitable. They're now our elder trees and if we're going to be paying attention to what God is saying through creation, these trees are a great place to start. They've survived 9/11, the Iraq war, Vietnam, World Wars II & I, the Spanish American war, the Civil War, and the European discovery and conquest of the Cascades. Every day, no matter who's in power, no matter what's on the front page to depress us, they *Just. Keep. Growing.* Can we also keep growing, come what may? Yes, if we can learn to be more like trees.

It all starts with receiving. The science is too much for this booklet, though for the curious, some of great books on the subject, along with a video, will help you go deeper.[12] The vital principle is that trees can only grow, give, and shelter others because of what they've first received.

A perfect combination of carbon dioxide, sunlight, water and rest create an ecosystem enabling each tree to produce the sugars and other nutrients they need for growth. If any of these elements are missing, everything comes to a halt. The tree won't be able to keep growing, and the only other option is death. The moral of the story should be clear enough: A tree cut off from the sources above will never fulfill its mission of multiplication, shelter, and blessing. The trees in

---

[12] The Hidden Life of Trees - Illustrated Edition; Peter Wohlleben; Greystone Books, 2015

Finding the Mother Tree: Discovering the Wisdom of the Forest; Suzanne Simmard; Alfred A. Knopf Publishers

The Secret Life of Trees (video) https://bit.ly/treelife56

our part of the world that are 600, 700, 800 years old (and more) have maintained this posture of receptivity for centuries, through all manner of weather, all threats, all natural disasters. Let this perfect cocktail of sunlight, water, and carbon dioxide work its magic, turning the chlorophyll into food for growth. The sun goes down. Rest. Repeat. Grow and bless the forest, and hence the entire planet, day after day, for centuries. That's the way it works, no matter what empire happens to be ruling, no matter what the church thinks about its most recent hot topic, no matter anything. Trees stay the course, doing what the Creator intended they do.

Central to our consideration is the fact that trees can't grow without a continual rhythm that includes receiving from above. We'd do well to learn from them because we can't either. Whether the Biblical author James is being literal or poetic, his word that "every good and perfect gift coming from above[13]" is intended to elevate our gaze. Too much of the time we allow ourselves to be stuck in the buying and selling, lusting and consuming, posturing and competing elements of life "under the sun." Yes, we *do* buy, desire, consume, and find our place in the world, but if we're to be on a trajectory toward increasing wholeness, these things always come *after* the first things, the things we receive, which form the foundation of our identity. This is a bit of what Jesus was talking about when he rebuked his hostess at a party for being worried about "so many things." He's not being rude. He's telling her that her productivity (and ours) will only be life-giving to us and fruitful for others when it comes out from a place of first receiving and being deeply rooted, connected with our Source of love and wholeness. We can't give what we don't have, and we'll only "have" in any

---

[13] James 1:17

sense that has value, to the extent that we practice the discipline of actively and consciously receiving God's gifts.

Almost every day, the vast majority of us receive an abundance of air, water, food, and weather. These gifts from above are our "starter," pack because without them we're dead. To this foundation, we're often able to add gifts of beauty, intimacy, encounters with creation. There are others too: joy, compassion, solidarity found in human contact, and bonuses that come to us when we're fortunate. These are gifts that uniquely bring us joy, gifts which vary by person and include coffee, tea, snow, warmth, rapids, fly fishing, Mozart, a three point shot at the buzzer, or any of a hundred other things.

There are invisible gifts too, and it's vital we name them, believe them, and keep them in our field of vision. For example, we can know we're forgiven, gifted, called, and empowered by our Creator. We know that we're never alone, because Jesus the Christ has promised to "never leave us our forsake us," no matter what we think or do. We'll doubt. We'll fail. We'll suffer. We'll shake our fist at heaven in rage perhaps. No matter our state, our Creator is always *with* us, always *for* us. Learning to believe this and live into it will be a key topic in our next chapter, but for the moment, know that these gifts are always here for us, raining down from above.

Receiving as a Lifestyle

When I inhale and say, "Christ above me" and then say "I receive" on the exhale, I'm giving myself the space to practice a conscious articulation of gratitude for the gifts I continually receive from my Creator. In the Bible, Paul names our lack of gratitude for the overwhelming abundance of gifts surrounding us as the core sin that sets humankind on a destructive path. In contrast, developing a habit of giving thanks every day for whatever gift is at the forefront of our awareness becomes a powerful force moving our lives upward into the realms of hope, joy, generosity, healing, and mercy.

Every day has its sorrows too, and some days the suffering and loss are overwhelming. Some pains come from unjust systems; others from the simple reality that because we live in fallen world, the arrows of illness, betrayal, and ultimately, death, will fall to us. We're at our best when we're present in the midst of it all, pouring out our hearts to God and walking the deep valleys with authentic grief and presence to our pain.

Still, the gifts keep raining down. Families impacted by cancer speak of Jesus showing up in the life of a nurse. Incarcerated individuals share stories of seeing clouds in the window and feeling a sense of wonder and gratitude. A soldier shares the beauty of an encounter with the enemy. That moment melted her weary heart due to their shared faith. And of course, we're still breathing, still tasting water, and the sun is still rising, miracles all! We all receive constantly. The question we face: do we even see, and if we do, is our response gratitude?

Christ above me. I receive your gifts constantly, regardless of whether I'm praising, cursing, or ignoring you. Thanks be to you that your faithful generosity is offered without conditions. Give me eyes to see, and the sense of wonder to respond with gratitude. Thank you.

Christ Above Me Practice:
Receive the Gifts

Cultivating a posture of receptivity to God's gifts is a journey that is largely determined by our ability to do two things: **pay attention** and **practice gratitude**. Oftentimes our inability to receive and respond to God is not for lack of trying, but rather a lack of noticing. We move quickly through the moments of our day, often carrying a multitude of burdens and a persistent voice that whispers, *"do more, do better"* on repeat.

The following practice is an invitation to embrace a less hurried and more attentive way. As we slow down and direct our minds to what is before us, we find God's gifts abound in the seemingly ordinary moments of our day.

Step One: Set aside five minutes each evening this week to reflect on your day. Find a quiet space and take a few deep breaths until you feel settled. If it helps, engage the encircling meditation until you feel present to what is happening in the moment.

Step Two: Continue breathing deeply, and begin to recall your day starting with the moment you woke up this morning. Did you wake feeling rested? Anxious? Excited for the day? There is no right or wrong answer except what was true to your experience.

Step Three: As you walk through the day, pay attention as God brings to mind people, experiences or feelings for which you are grateful. This could be something as small as a moment of quiet on your commute to work, an encouraging word from a friend or a grounding encounter with nature. Use the following pages to list these moments of gratitude.

* * *

Step Four: Once you have finished reflecting on the moments of your day, read each item on your list aloud, and then close the practice by praying the following:

God, I receive these gifts from you as an expression of your infinite goodness and love. Thank you for the multitude of ways your kingdom is breaking into this world and into my life. May I grow in my capacity to see and receive all that you give, as I learn to live joyfully in light of your abundance. Amen

Truth Two: Christ Beneath Me - I am Rooted

(May you be)… rooted and grounded in love. ~Paul the Apostle

* * *

*That person is like a tree firmly planted by streams of water, which yields its
fruit in season and whose leaf does not wither.* ~David the
Shepherd King

Learning from the Trees

Roots serve two significant purposes for trees. Of the first order, roots are grounding. Every tree faces countless storms over the course of its life. They survive by remaining firmly embedded in the life force that is its soil. Our house in the forest is full of fir and hemlock trees which are challenged by storms on a regular basis, assaulted by high winds, loaded down with heavy snow and ice, and more. If they're stiff they'll snap like a twig. The reason they remain for centuries is because flexibility enables them to bend, absorbing whatever loads or forces nature throws at them. The forces is transferred from needle to branch, to trunk, and finally down into the root. Down there, invisible to the rest of us, the energy is absorbed and dispersed into the soil, the final backstop against the ravages of storms. All this can happen because of the marvel that is a tree's roots.

Beyond the physics of it, roots offer a biological foundation too. Buried as they are in the depths of the nutrient-dense forest floor, they provide the conduit whereby the tree might gain all it needs to both fend off enemies and grow strong. From this place of robust health, it fulfills its place in the world as a source of shelter for the forest floor from the hot sun and pounding rain, a resting place for birds, *the* major means of capturing carbon, and our fundamental source of oxygen. You see why trees matter! Take away the roots and the trees are lost. Without trees, carbon sequestration and our source of oxygen is lost. For us, of course, if there's no oxygen all is lost! Roots are invisible, but as is often the case, what's below the surface and hidden is vital to all that's going on above ground.

As vital as roots are, more is needed if the life of a tree is to flourish. The soil is the storehouse of nutrients that roots draw upon to sustain their growth through seasons, years, and centuries. Roots, embedded in soil, actively draw from the resources of nitrogen, phosphorus, and other compounds essential to the tree's growth and health.

Think about this for a moment. Every bite of salad, every mouthful of wild or pastured protein we eat, every refreshing moment of shade we enjoy, every breath of oxygen-rich air we inhale - all of this comes to us from plants and trees, which thrive only to the extent that they have a healthy root system. Every moment of our lives we're the receiving sustenance sustenance because of the invisible and inglorious work of roots. We can ignore them and just enjoy the fruits, but plants can't. Without the roots, they're dead.

Root work, by its nature, is hidden work. Nobody's taking pictures of roots and displaying them on social media. There isn't a single root I'm aware of that has followers, or would be considered an "influencer." You'd never even know they exist if you only looked on the surface of things. However, in the springtime, "1 acre of grassland or pasture may have about 1,000 pounds of standing shoot mass aboveground but as much as 3,500 pounds of roots below ground, in the top foot of soil.[14]" This calculates to a 3.5 to 1 ratio of underground work to what's visible on the surface!

When it comes to the human soul, root work is hidden there too. Each of us has a visible above ground life: our vocation, family life, and the responsibilities and joys we embrace as parent, child, spouse, friend, neighbor, creator, athlete, musician. These parts of our lives are on display and

---

[14] https://www.noble.org/news/publications/ag-news-and-views/2018/june/why-roots-matter-to-soil-plants-and-you/

provide the chance for immediate, but not always accurate, feedback. People tell us we're OK, or not OK, based on their own limited perceptions and bent opinions. Feedback matters, but if our lives are primarily shaped by what others say about us, we're headed for trouble. Many are assessing our decisions, priorities, and values from the vantage point of their own wisdom and pain, triumph and suffering, love and rejection. As a result, human feedback can be fickle: sometimes spot-on, and others times wildly inaccurate. If we live and die by it, we'll eventually die by it. Not literally, perhaps, but our sense of security, clear conscience, sense of calling, capacity to serve out from a place of love; these elements will suffer harm and loss every time. We can't live our public lives on the basis of human feedback alone. If we do, we'll become reactionary and ultimately won't survive the storms.

There's a better way.

Rooted and Grounded in Love

The soil in which you and I are invited to be deeply rooted and firmly grounded is our identity in Christ. We walk through our days as trees. Storms arise unannounced, and our souls are battered by the winds of lies declaring our inadequacy as settled fact. "Not good enough, disciplined enough, pure enough, rich enough, sensitive enough, courageous enough, loving enough, faithful enough, healthy enough, young enough."

God knows there are plenty of voices telling us we're inadequate, some loud and direct, others more subtle. To the extent that we believe these lies we're at risk of derailing our calling by wallowing in shame. Sometimes we add to our woes by making terrible choices to self-medicate the pain of shame in destructive ways, or we just become angry cynics whose vision for living a meaningful life withers like a tree who's roots are dead.

Unless we're well rooted, these winds will topple us, and we'll find ourselves functionally cut off from the source of all that is good and life-giving for our souls. Your roots are the "ground truths" of who your Creator has declared you to be "in Christ." These are our deepest reality, and by being rooted in them, we'll withstand the storms of life and continue on with our calling to grow, serve, and bless our broken and thirsty world. This works beautifully, because every storm is an opportunity for you to become more firmly rooted. Are you anxious? You simply remind yourself that Christ is your *peace*. Are you facing fear? Christ is your *courage*. Anger? Christ is your *patience*.

This plays out simply and practically. I'm feeling weak and inadequate for whatever reason, as I wait to get up and give a talk. I simply pray, "I receive your strength Lord. Thank you." I may pray this simple prayer five or six times, and I find that each time I pray, my breathing will slow a bit, to the point I can usually feel a physiological difference in the state of my body. I've moved away from the fight/flight mode that needlessly characterizes too many of my waking hours. Instead, the "peace of Christ, which is beyond all understanding[15]" is beginning to take hold.

When Paul the Apostle prayed for us, though, he didn't pray that we'd be "rooted and grounded in *Christ*", but that we'd be "rooted and grounded in *love*[16]." Our invitation is to be bathed in the knowledge and conviction that our Creator is infinitely, irrevocably, and relentlessly *for* us. There are winds of deception blowing, telling us that we're not enough

---

[15] Philippians 4:7
[16] Ephesians 3:17

because we don't measure up to some cultural or religious standards. Doing root work gives you the capacity to flex when battered by these lies as you learn to consistently draw from the resources of Christ's life and what God says about you. This flexibility and rootedness exists as an ecosystem, meaning *both* are needed. Here's why:

Flexibility

It's in us to have expectations and hopes regarding how things will go in our lives. Reality often tells a different story though. Traffic conditions, the oncologist's report, spousal infidelity or abuse, or accidents on the freeway are just some of a million ways dissonance between our expectations and reality are manifest. We thought it would be this way, and instead it's another, far less pleasant, way. Disappointments are inevitable. How we react isn't. We have freedom to choose our response and our choice will become a major determinant of our future.

We might be tempted to think the healthiest response is to put on a happy face or "make the best of it", declaring "God is good all the time." As a pastor who's been present with people who've held their dead child in their arms or watched their girlfriend get swept away and buried in an avalanche, I can tell you that these kinds of hollow praise responses aren't the way of wisdom. Part of healing and intimacy with God is having the courage to mourn the dissonance, loss, and reality that our world is desperately broken. Just read Psalm 23. The valley of shadows and death is a real part of our journey.

Mourning at its healthiest, though, doesn't mean we scream at God and walk away. Instead, we lament in the same way deciduous trees behave in autumn; we let go of that which needs to fall away; we flex with realities of unforeseen storms; we remain rooted in the truth that God *loves* us and is *for* us. Through these experiences we are learning to draw deeply on the resources of Christ's life as our basis of sustenance in the midst of darkness and loss.

Much of the suffering we experience in our lives comes from our expectations that life is formulaic. Insert "x" (hard work, prayer, obedience, giving, moral purity) and you'll get "y" (success, marriage, family, promotion, health). Everyone has their own variables for "x" and "y", but the formula is there. It's part of the domination model that presumes human capacity for control. We mistakenly believe that with enough effort, planning, and discipline, we can control outcomes.

Here's the ground truth that should drive us to our Creator every day:
Control is an illusion.

Rooted people embrace their lack of control in the same way trees embrace storms:

I don't know what my financial future will be.

I don't know how long I'll live, or how I'll die.

I don't know if those who admire me today will disdain me tomorrow.

I don't know if my spouse will die before or after me.

I don't know the future stability or longevity of my country.

I don't know how the warming planet will affect my grandchildren's future.

There aren't enough empty notebooks in the world to write down all that we don't know or can't know. Far from depressing, embracing this truth becomes liberating because it turns our focus to what we *can* know, and that's where we become rooted.

We can know that in this fallen world, things won't always

go the way we hope. We can know there'll be what Isaiah the prophet calls fires, and that they'll be inescapable for us. We'll need to walk through them. But we *can* know God's promise, which is that "when you walk through the fire, I will be with you[17]."

This, in the end, is the hope of the gospel. Instead of immunity, we're promised something better: Christ's power, presence, and perseverance in the midst of whatever comes our way. We can know we're not alone. We can know we're loved unconditionally, even though we'll doubt, and stumble, and fall. These knowings will both release us from the tyranny of unrealistic expectations for our lives to unfold perfectly and grant us contentment in the companionship of Christ. When Christ becomes enough, and a true companion, we'll mourn, but not as those without hope. As one who's known plenty of loss in my six-plus decades of living, I can testify that this is both true and the primary reason I keep drinking from the waters of Christ's life.

Feeding on Resources

The quiet confidence of this companionship is what allows me to flex in the storms. But this confidence develops slowly through consistent habits of meditating on what God says about me. Jesus said that our primary battle in this world boils down to whether we believe truths or lies, and the most fundamental truths we need to learn to embrace, are the ones God says about us. Here are just a few:

God is for us (Romans 8:31)
   God isn't angry (I John 2:1-2)
   God has adopted us into God's eternal family (Ephesians

---

[17] Isaiah 43:2

1:5)

God has given us every spiritual blessing (Ephesians 1:3)

God has created each of us with a unique purpose (Ephesians 2:10)

God has given us everything we need to live the life we're created to live (II Peter 1:3)

Perhaps most important of all: *Nothing can ever separate us from the love of God*[18]. This means that we have the possibility of relationship that has no contingencies. Our relationship with God isn't predicated on performance, or circumstances, or obedience because unconditional love is God's character. We don't necessarily feel this way about God, and no doubt have a hard time believing it to be true, at least sometimes. Part of the reason for this is because that kind of infinite, unconditional love can't be found, at least not in its purest form, between humans. Relationships feel fragile to us, even the best of them at times for various reasons, including the reality that people die too soon and intimacy is torn from us. To be rooted and grounded in love is to know, in that part of our being that's deeper than circumstances or emotions, that there's one who will never leave us, whose love for us is without condition, into whose arms we can always run. Knowing that our Creator loves us in this stable, infinite, lavish way means we have peace, and when have peace, our roots are deep, deep enough even to weather the storms which batter humans.

I think of a friend in Rwanda who lost 153 family members to the genocide in 1994. He's spent most of his career mediating reconciliation between genocide victims and perpetrators. If he were to jump out of the pages of this booklet right now and talk to you, he'd tell you that he's

---

[18] Romans 8:31-39

healed from bitterness and hate, strengthened to move into a work he'd never have chosen, and given steady joy in the midst of ongoing setbacks and challenges. And he'd tell you that all that comes from one source: "I've been rooted in God's infinite love for me, and for every tribe and nation. I know God's love for all of us. Discovering this, and believing this, has changed everything for me."

Christ beneath me: I am rooted in your love, a love which is true, real, and unchanging, in spite of the fact that I change. I move from doubt to faith, anxiety to peace, rage to acceptance, cynicism to hope. Thank you, Creator God, for your declaration that through all the storms, both those I create through my own foolishness and those that hit me just by living in a fallen world, your love remains the single constant unshakeable source. May I learn to believe it, receive it, and be increasingly rooted in it as days turn to years and decades. Thank you.

"Christ Beneath Me" Practice: Identity Truths

Many of us long to be rooted in our truest identity in Christ, yet we struggle to remain in this place of grounded assurance. The cultural scripts around us locate our worth in status, body conformity, wealth, and certain expressions of intelligence. The messaging we absorb on social media and elsewhere often reinforces these scripts. How easily we find ourselves controlled by the need for more in order to prove our worth and value.

The following practice is an invitation to daily situate ourselves in the ultimate and definitive truth of who God says that we are. As we learn to live in this place of beloved assurance, we find ourselves less caught up in the domination model, and more available to freely and confidently respond to God's leading.

Step One: Find a place where you can be in silence for the next ten minutes. Take a few deep breaths and bring your attention to the here and now. As you breathe in say "Christ Beneath Me" and as you breathe out say, "I am rooted." Continue with this breath prayer until you feel present to the moment.

Step Two: When you feel ready, slowly begin to read through the identity truths on the following page. Consider inserting your name as you read a particular truth. For instance instead of reading "I am Beloved," try saying, "Richard is beloved."

Step Three: Read through the identity truths a second time and pay attention to any affirmation that catches your attention. Circle that truth.

Step Four: Look back at the identity truths you've circled and consider why the Holy Spirit may have directed you to this particular truth. Is it something you doubt? Something you need to embrace today? Something that speaks to a particular life circumstance you are facing?

Step Five: Choose one of the circled affirmations and write it on a sticky note, scrap of paper or journal. Ideally, you record this identity truth somewhere you will be reminded of it throughout your day as a way to deepen your roots in the soil of Christ's love.

Truth Three: Christ Around Me - I'm Connected

If you help individual trees by getting rid of their supposed competition, the remaining trees are bereft. They send messages out to the their neighbors in vain, because nothing remains but stumps...there are now a lot of losers in the forest. Weaker members who would otherwise have been supported by the stronger ones, suddenly fall behind...a tree can only be as strong as the forest that surrounds it[19].
~Peter Wohlleben

I have been to many countries and seen much poverty and

---

[19] The Hidden Life of Trees - Illustrated Edition; Peter Wohlleben; Greystone Books, 2015; p26

suffering. But of all the countries I have been to, the poorest one is America... (because) America suffers from the poverty of loneliness.
~Mother Teresa

If one member suffers, all suffer together; if one member is honored,

all rejoice together.

~I Corinthians 12:26

Learning from the Trees: Forest or the Bonsai?

I was once a fan of bonsai trees. They stand alone, nourished only by their care giver, who must trim both branches and roots with consistency and accuracy. It must be watered with precision, and the tiny volume of soil must be fortified in order to provide the right nutrients for its highly un-natural environment. There are a few bonsai trees that are 500 years old, so I was intrigued enough with the art form that I tried, unsuccessfully, to care for and sustain two different bonsais.

I'm finished now. I spent a decent part of the pandemic season watching documentaries and listening to podcasts about forests and trees, discovering along the way that it is both unnatural and unhealthy for any tree to live alone. There's a give and take of nutrients, a sharing of carbon, and embedded communication systems among the trees to warn each other of impending danger. What's more, lots of resource and information-sharing happens not only through entwined root systems, but through the mycelium network, that vast web of fungi woven tightly throughout the forest floor. Like humans, it's now apparent that trees are made for community.

Because my own story includes adoption (which carries an element of abandonment), coupled with the untimely death of my adoptive dad, followed by my sister's death at the early age of 43, I've tended toward individualism rather than community. It's been a survival mechanism. "Nobody can promise to be there for you" became a mantra. There's truth in the statement, so my mantra wasn't all bad, in my opinion. My sense is that I sometimes enjoy a reality of intimacy with our invisible God that others struggle to find. Perhaps this is because I've clung to the reality of God as the one unchanging source of hope in my life; my rock; my fortress; my high tower. I'll hide myself in God and there be safe from all the dying, abandonment, and betrayal that comes with inevitable losses that happen in this world. It sounded good to me at 23 and still has a strong element of appeal now in my senior years, because it feels bombproof. I tell people that I never travel alone, that Christ is my constant companion, and I mean it. Christ is enough.

And yet... It's not the whole truth, or at least not the most accurate expression of truth. One of the most effective sermons I ever preached included a film clip from "A Beautiful Day in the Neighborhood." I shared that moment when Mr. Rogers asks his guests to think about people who'd invested in them: teachers, coaches, parents, pastors maybe. I put it in the sermon because when I sat in the theater and actually did that, a long parade of 'investors in me' passed before my mind's eye: Adoptive parents, a music teacher from high school, an architecture student from college days, three different pastors offering three different life-changing sermons, two seminary professors, a pastor from seminary days, and on and on it went. WOW! I realized that the good that's coming out of my life is not solely "of my own making." I'm who I am because of the grace, generosity, affirmation, love, and encouragement of countless souls rained down on me. It took a whole village to create me, and you too.

It's theologically accurate to quote Psalm 73, as I like to do. It reads, regarding God, "Whom have I in heaven but You, and having You, I desire nothing else on earth." For decades I misinterpreted that to mean "I don't need anyone - ever." While I've been grateful to have experienced real intimacy with Jesus, I'm now able to see that the extent to which I've tried to go it alone has actually impoverished my life. Like all trees, I'm made for community.

Besides fanning the flames of individualism, my "go it alone" mindset had the untidy effect of creating insensitivity. Others would be in need, and I'd say to myself, "They don't need me. They have Jesus," and get back to whatever it was I was doing. Only after taking up the mantle of leadership in a Seattle church which had a covert motto of "tangling our heartstrings together" did I begin to fully experience and embrace the value of community.

It came about from seeing it firsthand. Young couples where one spouse was battling cancer would be upheld by their close network of friends. Mothers of preschoolers would gather bi-weekly to share the challenges and joys of parenting. As couples grew old together they'd celebrate and mourn over each others' successes and losses, support each other for their children's weddings, or walk through deep valleys of losing a spouse. Along the way, job changes, moral failures, hidden addictions coming to the light, retirement parties, trips overseas to support partners in ministry, laughter around campfires, and so much more has been on display to testify of this simple reality: *We were never meant to go it alone.*

Connections as Lifestyle

For many of us in this highly individualized, "DIY" western world, connection with others remains mostly theory unless we take steps to weave our lives together with others.

This requires time and intentionality. Most significantly, we must move away from sentimental notions of being connected with others, and embrace the real work and joy of relationship. This can begin with our meditation. As I say "Christ around me. I am Connected" I allow the spirit of God to bring to mind various people in my life. In one breath, it might be a co-worker, and next time a family member. Then a neighbor, or recreational companion, or someone with whom I volunteer. I might recall a friend working on the front lines to address homelessness, or a friend who works in ER for brain trauma.

Whoever God brings to mind, I offer a prayer of thanks for them, even when the person who comes to mind is "difficult." The prevailing domination model that puts people into categories of either "ally" or "threat" is unsustainable when this pattern of praying takes hold. That worn out binary way of viewing humanity dissolves and in its place every person becomes a neighbor. Committing people to God's care in this way frees us from our need to control others. Their behavior and responses to us are no longer our responsibility so we're free to love and serve unconditionally. It's liberating to us and dignifying to the other.

Over time, it becomes apparent in many cases that there's more to be done than simply prayer. God brings to mind practical next steps I can take to serve, encourage, reconcile, bles. There are a number of "one another" exhortations in the Bible that offer practical steps we can take to deepen our connections. Here are two:

Serve One Another

The American poverty of loneliness Mother Teresa spoke of doesn't imply that we don't have parties to attend, scores of 'friends' on social media, and very full calendars. For most of us, we have all these. Those connections aren't the point though. The question is, who will be there for you when there's been domestic violence? In whom do you confide when you've made a huge mistake? When you hit rock bottom because health challenges force a loss of work and income, who walks that road with you? Who knows the you that exists behind the public veil?

In every case, the answer will be "those who are willing to serve others," which has nothing to do with how many parties you attend. It's about whether you see "the other" in your life as someone worth the investment of time, money, and emotional energy. For too many of us, our plates are so full of pursuits having to do with our own well-being that we've nothing left for those in need. As a result, many are fighting great battles alone.

Those who see with the *eyes* of Jesus will be empowered to respond with the *heart* of Jesus, and when this happens, they will become servants. They'll all be serving different people in different ways, following in the footsteps of the one who had room in his life for disruption and unanticipated opportunities for service.

Encourage One Another

One of life's transformative conversations for me came while studying architecture. I'd been both healed and transformed by the ministry of encouragement a fellow student had imparted to me over and over again. We lived in the same dorm and he affirmed my gifts of music, my calling in architecture, and my faith in Christ, fragile and tentative as it had become after the recent death of my dad. I'll never forget what he said when I asked him why he seemed to go out of his way to be so affirming of everyone. "Most people already know where they fall short in their lives. There are plenty of people willing to point that out. But there aren't many people pointing out where other people are doing right, or what natural talents they have. People need that and I can give it, so I do."

So did Jesus. So can you. That's the ministry of encouragement.

The forest I live in is presently facing all kinds of challenges due to shorter winters and drier, warmer summers. More than ever, each tree needs what the other has to offer if they are, together, going to survive the challenges of this present age. The good news is that they've survived before: climate cycles, fires, heavy snow years, drought years, and more. Through it all, for millennia, the forests just keep going, and growing. "How do they do that?" you ask. Together! "For as in one body we have many members, and the members do not all have the same function, so we, though many, are one body in Christ, and individually members one of another." (Romans 12:4,5)

Christ around me. I'm connected to every member of Your body, and in a larger sense, to the whole family of humanity, each image-bearers of God. Grant that I might have eyes to see my connection with each person, to the end that I might serve and encourage and give and receive, weaving my life into the fabric of the other lives You bring my way. Though it will require energy and risk and some pain, no doubt, I believe it is Your desire and far, far better than being a Bonsai. Take me there by Your grace. Thank you.

"Christ Around Me" Practice: Hospitality

The practice of hospitality is one way we give and receive the love of Christ through connection with others. In Benedictine monasticism, hospitality means a "call to openness." We develop eyes to see others as the person of Christ, and open our own lives to them the same way we would open ourselves to Christ.

Depending on circumstances this might mean opening our homes, our wallets, our hearts, our minds, our refrigerators... whatever we have to be used for God's redemptive purposes.

Step One: Take a few minutes to quiet and focus your mind. Ask God to bring to mind people for whom He'd like you to pray. When God brings a name to mind, simply write that name down. As you record the name, pray this simple prayer: ***"God, may your peace be upon _____ today. Direct their path toward your good end."*** Pray this prayer for each person on your list.

Step Two: When you finish your few minutes of prayer, look over the list of names and ask for the Holy Spirit's guidance to identify one person you might show hospitality toward today. Circle that name on your list. Remember, the practice of hospitality means to open your life to that person in a way that blesses them. The point is not to "fix" them, but rather to connect with them.

Step Three: Consider the person you've circled. What do they need right now? How might you open up your life to them in service today? How might this act be a step in the direction of connection? It could be as simple as a phone call, text message or a handwritten letter. Below are some ideas, but feel free to come up with your own!

* * *

- Set up a Happy Hour or Dinner with them. Create a series of fun questions to facilitate meaningful connection.

- Purchase a gift card from a local business and send it to them by mail with a word of encouragement.

- Make a meal or sweet treat, or pick up something from a coffee shop, and drop it off at their door.

- Call them and ask how you can pray for them.

- Share a memory or photo of a time or place you both enjoy.

Truth Four: Christ Within Me - I am Called

No matter how unimportant we feel ourselves to be, we can pulsate with divine energy and have an unshatterable confidence that Christ is in action as we depend on him. ~Major Ian Thomas

How shall we picture the kingdom of God, or by what parable shall we present it? It is like a mustard seed, which, when sown upon the soil, though it is smaller than all the seeds that are upon the soil, yet when it is sown, it grows up and becomes larger than all the garden plants and forms large branches; so that the birds of the air can nest under its shade ~Jesus the Christ

* * *

Don't ask what the world needs. Ask what makes you come alive and go do it, because what the world needs is people who have come alive. ~anonymous

Learning from the Trees: Made for Regeneration

As I write this I'm sitting outside, in a mountain forest east of Seattle. On the best weather days, this is my outdoor office. I look down and begin counting how many baby trees there are within my sight line. I stop at 100 when I realize trying to find an accurate number is folly. There are too many new lives to count. The moment is undeniable evidence of this basic creation law: Life creates life[20]. Though it wouldn't be obvious if you were quickly hiking, if you stop and pay attention, you discover there's a generation of infant trees at your feet throughout most of the forest. They are the future and they exist because life is doing what it's made to do: generating more life!

This is wholly unspectacular work. Cones fall from fir trees and take their place in the soil where a process of the shell decaying ultimately releases the life inside. That life begins a relationship of symbiosis with the soil so that, fortified with the right temperature, nutrients, and moisture, cell division begins and life multiplies, continuously, until a new tree germinates. Fast forward a few hundred years and some of these new trees will be mature, profoundly contributing to

---

[20] As a pastor, I'm aware of the pain of infertility or singleness and what a jarring statement this might be for those who've walked what feel like barren roads. Without taking anything away from such pain, it's vital that we see that "life" here is beyond biology. The life we're called to birth into the world is birthed as joy, peace, healing, justice, hope, and generosity. Others are living fuller lives because Christ in us has been released to be Christ for them. This is the promise of life we can all claim.

the health of the forest and the planet as was God's design, and become a new source of life! All life is made for regenerative purposes. For many, "new life" happens well beyond the boundaries of physical biology and its that broader vision of life that we now consider.

Jesus uses both biological and erotic imagery to drive home the point that humans are made for reproduction. He calls us branches connected to the life that is his vine, and tells us that as such, we're made to be fruitful, which is to say that we're made to bring light, hope, justice, compassion, and healing to people and places where it's been missing. He uses erotic language when he calls we who follow him 'the bride.' As the groom, he fills us with his divine life (remember that imagery in Colossians 1:26-28: "Christ in you, the hope of glory"). We receive his seed, and as his life enters and unites with ours, we become those who pour all the goodness that is Christ into our parched world.

The remarkable truth is that we're invited to live in mysterious union with Christ. The result of such union will be the fruit of divine life born through us, a theme woven across the pages of the Bible. God promised Abraham that the world would be blessed through him. God used Esther to bless and save an oppressed people from genocide by birthing justice in the midst of what would have otherwise been unbridled destruction. The thread that began in the Bible has become a full blown tapestry through the centuries. Hospitals. Leper colonies. Shelters for the unhoused. Addiction treatment centers. Immigrant advocacy. Bach. Galileo. Harriet Tubman and the Underground Railroad. For every known name and cause like these there are millions, billions maybe, whose fruit was less visible, but no less real. "The army of the anonymous" as a friend once said, is doing most of the work, and most of the work, like the birthing of these trees, is wholly unspectacular.

Scattered across generations, classes, nations, and abilities, there have always been people giving birth to the kingdom of God's good reign. Mostly, it's practicing immense patience with infants, caring for the needs of an elder, living simply and giving the rest away, or throwing parties for neighbors and letting the candles burn low while people share their stories and learn they can be heard, and known deeply, and still loved. This is the fruit that never makes the headlines or becomes a movie, and yet it is the core God's work in the world. These ordinary lives ripen to a fine wine. I've met quiet saints doing the ordinary work of faithfulness and have come to believe that those are the lives which, like the forests of the world, are keeping the rest of us alive. Take "Christ in you" out of the army of the anonymous, and our species, if not the entire planet, will sink into unbridled greed, violence, lust, fear, and cynicism. This is because, as Genesis says, "sin is crouching at the door" just waiting to sink us all. All we need do in order to live horrible lives, is follow the path of least resistance. Perhaps that is part of the reason that Jesus called the path of those following him the 'narrow road.'

The entryway to the broad road is only appealing because we've lost sight of (or never discovered) our truer, higher, calling and identity. Failing to see and embrace God's invitation to abundant life, the lights near the broad, wide open gate to the carnival of consumption and individualism look appealing enough that we're drawn in, and soon find ourselves caught in a cycle of work, debt, comparison, and destructive self-medicating comforts, all of which conspire to make life more burden than blessing.

The alternative? Take up your calling to be a *blessing* in the world. Find your gifts and share them freely. There's a word for this kind of life:

Freedom and Abundance

In some places, freedom is defined as "freedom to do whatever you want" which leads to arguments in America about things like owning guns, wearing a mask during a pandemic, building a house that blocks my neighbor's view, reframing my sexual ethic any way I want, and much more. Underlying these conversations is a fundamental question about how much any government should be able to intrude into a person's life, and debates ensue.

This can't be the freedom Jesus is speaking of, though, because his promises aren't contingent on a libertarian form of government, nor did he speak of democracy, republic, woke, or cancel culture. Instead, he declares true freedom to be a byproduct of continuing in Jesus' word. For those that do so, there's this promise: "You will know the truth and the truth will set you free[21]."

He goes on to define freedom as our capacity to overcome the slavery which ensues when we're sucked into the cultural carnival of comparison and consumption spoken of earlier. Jesus says that everyone who sins becomes a 'slave to sin,' by which he means that we find ourselves first seduced by, then stuck in the carnival with seemingly no way out. We may look with disgust at the world of oppression, addiction, pathological loneliness, and income inequity that's all around us, but we've not a clue what to do about it, or worse: we know what's needed from us, but can't find the courage to take the next step. As a result we feel trapped, even though in our clearest moments of insight we know the carnival and its trivial social media debates are smoke and mirrors, distracting us from the real darkness, and the real source of hope. The choices we make in such a state are not good.

---

[21] John 8:32

While we might find momentary comfort in the next binge series to watch, or the next purchase, or even the next cause *"di' jour,"* those who stop and pay attention to their hearts are faced with the sense that life around us and within us is deeply flawed. This is what Jesus means when he speaks of being slaves to sin.

Jesus' freedom comes about because those living out from the wisdom and power of Christ are able to increasingly align their lives with something better. This capacity comes as a promise without contingency, and has been demonstrated from the streets of Selma, to the Gulag of Russia, from the boardrooms of New York City, to rural oncology wards, to the shanties of South Africa. Make no mistake about it: While God cares about freedom from political oppression, the foundation of freedom begins with Christ's life filling us, aligning our lives with his, being filled with the Holy Spirit and, as a result, stepping into the story of hope God is writing in the world.

Jesus says "remaining in my word" is the portal through which we enter into this kind of freedom. This is where meditation comes in. To remain can be translated "to abide" which essentially means "to be at home in." That phrase makes sense to us in the 21st century because we all have home pages on our phones and laptops. They're usually pictures of things that delight us: spouses, children, a favorite sunset memory, our dog. They "take us home" to what matters most.

What matters most to you? Jesus is inviting us to become, in the best sense of the word, *obsessed* with him and his view of the world because he is the true and lasting source of peace, justice, forgiveness, grace, truth, hope, and mercy. Because Christ lives *in* us, and we increasingly believe that to be true, we'll begin to see the world with Jesus' eyes, to feel the pain of the world with his heart, to respond as his spirit-empowered hands and feet. This, Jesus says, is what happens when his life becomes our home page. To the extent this new home page becomes our bedrock defining reality, a life of binge watching, eating, buying, or binge anything, is no longer appealing. Instead, we begin seeing these things for the cheap escapes from reality that they are. We find ourselves, over time (and usually with a few setbacks along the way), increasingly freed from those indulgences that once defined us. Freed indeed!

A key insight here is that our freedom doesn't come from killing desire. It's less a picture of doing battle with the seductive sirens of ice cream and alcohol, sexual conquest and sunshine by the pool, and more about being captured by the eternal beauty of Christ and the story of hope God desires to write in this world. As one person said to me when coming to Christ, "If Jesus is about giving dignity to the poor, replacing wars with eternal peace, learning to forgive and love enemies, and throwing a party for those on the margins, I'm in!" She quickly added, "But who knew?" telling me that her previous understanding of Christ-followers was that they were political partisans who didn't care about the poor, immigrants, the environment, or people who didn't fit a narrow culturally devised ethical construct of the world.

Her confusion makes sense, because we're still in the thick of a 100 year old civil war among Christ followers. The debate hinges on what "freedom in Christ" means. Some see freedom as wholly internal; Christ freeing people from the enslavement and affects of personal sins. Others focus on Jesus' more expansive declarations and demonstrations of freedom. He crossed social divides. He demonstrated a kingdom in which slaves are set free, woman are empowered, those living on the margins are dignified. In Jesus' kingdom, everyone has a place at the table! Some, focused on this external 'new kingdom' freedom, ignore the call to personal transformation and freedom. But without freedom from our own propensity for self-destructive choices, we're stuck in the carnival. Others ignore the expansive freedom, believing that Jesus' main interest is in getting everyone's ticket punched for a new eternal destination called heaven. Throughout the 20th century and into the next, the debate was largely framed as between conservatives (personal transformation) and liberals (systemic transformation).

That debate is well beyond the scope of this little booklet, but there's the reality. When Jesus said, *"if the son shall make you free, you shall be free indeed,"* he wasn't 'either/or', he was 'both/and.' Systemic freedoms that come from dismantling things like slavery and nationalistic regimes such as Naziism began with inward heart transformation[22]. And any heart work we do that liberates us from the chains of a secret sexual addiction, or a shopping problem, or anger issue, any of that work must eventually create a spaciousness in my heart so that I now have both the capacity and clear conscience needed to serve our broken world. How do I know that? Jesus taught it! *"Freely you have received. Freely give."* In other words, to the extent that you've been blessed, remember that your blessing is intended to be passed on to others. You're here to birth new life!

Christ within me. I am called to bless and serve this broken world, called to be fruitful, which means allowing the seed of Christ's life within me to be received and nurtured in such a way that it germinates. The nature of that fruit, it's timing and it's size, is not my prerogative and hence not my concern.

---

[22] William Wilberforce's convictions regarding slavery changed after coming to Christ. Dietrich Bonhoeffer's stance against the Nazi regime in Germany stemmed from his naming the spiritual idol of nationalism.

Believing that Christ's life dwells within me in union with my humanity *is* my responsibility and to the extent that I embrace that reality, a shift will happen in me. I'll begin to see myself as the presence of Jesus in the world, and take up my mantle more willingly, even eagerly sometimes, as I embrace the joyful and challenging adventure of serving this broken world in Jesus name. Thanks be to you, O God, for this incredible gift!

"Christ Within Me" Practice:
Service

Though service may look different at each phase and stage of our lives, the call is still the same and the message remains: *As God's people, we live to embody the presence of Christ in the midst of brokenness, this is Christ within us!*

Scripture emphasizes that when we feed the hungry, stand against injustice, empower the vulnerable and serve the marginalized we are challenging, dismantling and transforming the domination model into a world where God's peace, beauty and flourishing reign. Thus, the practice of service is not simply about "doing good," but about participating in a much larger story of hope that Jesus is writing in the world.

Step One: Take a moment to consider the following truths of biblical service. How does this affirm or challenge your understanding of service?

Service is a privilege, not a chore (Gal 5:13; Matt 5:16; Matt 22:37).

Service is an invitation from God, to simply be myself in participation with what Christ is doing in the world (John

15:12; Heb 13:16).

Service goes both ways; it becomes an integral part of who we are and the communities we belong to (Gal 6:2; Phil 2:4).

Step Two: Take a moment and reflect on where you see need around you. What does need look like in your family? In your neighborhood? In your church? In your city? Feel free to use the following blank pages to brainstorm.

Step Three: Now make a second list, this one identifying the unique gifts and resources you have to offer the world at this season in your life. This list might include things like time, a dog who brings people joy, baking skills, business savviness, a car, or physical health.

Step Four: Consider your two lists. Where is there alignment? How might you use your gifts and resources to meet a need in your specific context? Feel free to bring others into this brainstorming process! This could be anything from planting a tree in your neighborhood to volunteering in your local school. Come up with two ways you would like to embody service in the coming weeks.

Afterword

I'm out walking my dog just as the sun comes up from behind the mountains near my home. As I write the Western USA is on fire, northern Germany is drowning under a flood, there's a coup in Haiti, and the pandemic crisis is getting worse in England, Asia and many states here at home. There's plenty to steal my joy, and those are just the big things. There are several more mini-crises, more personal, and unworthy of headlines, but serving up anxiety nonetheless. It's weighing on me. It leaves me wondering how to have honest hope and peace in the midst of this kind of world. What's more, I know many thoughtful people who feel this same sense of dis-ease, often with even greater intensity. Where do I find hope? How do I impart hope, call people to hope, in the midst of all that is our world? That's the backdrop of my morning walk.

As my dog and I hit the trail around the pond, shafts of

light from the rising sun fall on the mountains across the valley in a time frame that feels mysteriously like slow motion. The wall of fir trees clothing the mountainside grows lighter, imperceptibly and yet inevitably, welcoming the dawn with a multicolored doxology of illumination. As the waking continues, each moment becomes a festival of transformation. The light sets life in motion: bees awake, who take up visitation with the fireweed, daisies, foxglove, wild strawberries, salmonberries and more. A heron takes flight from the south end of the pond where water flows out to the creek. Within moments wind has invited the trees to a morning hoedown and they respond by dancing to the lead of the breeze. The hillside is a riot of color, motion, sound, scent.

I breathe the fir-saturated air. It's more, much more, beauty than I can absorb. Every morning "Life Wins" I say to myself while lifting my hands in a prayer of gratitude. This morning's liturgy of creation reminds me that Christ, who "holds all things together" is the deepest eternal reality. He's more real than the Declaration of Independence, Marshall Plan, Magna Carta, Doctrine of Discovery, or any of the other millions of documents that have been used to build nation states, economies, philosophies, and yes, religions too. Muslim, atheist, Buddhist, Christian, Capitalist, Socialist, Green Party, Republican, Democrat; the sun comes up for us all. The rains water the earth for us all. The trees give all of us oxygen. Native Americans call this the 'gift economy' and it will continue giving perpetually without regard to class, race, or ideology, at least until we destroy it. Everyone living receives these gifts.

After his arrest Jesus was questioned by the Governor of Judea, who had the power to free or execute him. He asked Jesus: "What have you done?" (wondering what crime he'd committed) and its important to connect the dots between

Jesus' answer and my morning sunrise worship session.

"My kingdom is not of this world[23]" is what Jesus said in response, and quickly added that if it were of this world, his disciples would have taken up arms and fought to save his life. But they didn't and he gave himself up without a fight because his authority was, as he reiterated, "of another realm" and he said it with an unnerving confidence as if Jesus believed his kingdom would continue, regardless of this trial's outcome, which is exactly what happened.

Too often Jesus' "not of this world" kingdom has been taken to mean solely something for a different time (the future), and different place (heaven). That doesn't work, though, because Jesus, speaking in his here (on earth) and now (present moment) said, "the kingdom of God is among you[24]" and alternatively "within you." Jesus went to great lengths to show us that nations will rise and fall. Economic systems will too. There'll always be an issue *di jour*. Sometimes it will be really important, like ending present day slavery, or restoring dignity to the heart that beats in the womb, or elevating the conversation about a planet on fire because of overconsumption. Of course these things matter, and a hundred other issues too.

And yet, while we squabble and seek to settle matters, gain power, keep power, and fight our battles, Jesus is keyed into an entirely different reality. Search the Bible. He said remarkably little about the corruption of the Roman Empire, or the hot button issues of oppression. Maybe it was because he knew that no matter which side ends up winning various territorial or culture wars, unless hearts are won, it won't make any ultimate difference. People will find ways to work around the rules, and ways oppress, dominate and be greedy.

---

[23] John 18:36
[24] Luke 17:21

It happened after the civil war ended in America, and the genocide in Rwanda. The camps are closed in Germany but anti-Semitism is still here. All this has to do with kingdoms of this world. They'll mutate, and in their best iterations might even evolve upwardly a bit. Still, Jesus makes it clear that these temporary kingdoms, called nations, are not and never will be, the deepest fundamental reality.

Jesus knows nations come and go, knows empires rise and fall, including those on the current roster of nations and empires. He knows economic systems mutate and evolve, sometimes upwardly and sometimes descending into chaos. He knows how vaporous and fleeting all this is, so he doesn't spend much time on these things. His main message is a deeper truth: "There's an eternal reality that transcends nations, systems, philosophies, and religions. This deeper truth is healing, beautiful, just, reconciling, peaceful, celebratory, and beautiful. And it's here. Now. Above you. Beneath you. Around you. Within you."

"Yes, but I forget."

Me too. We live in a world where thick veils hide the reality of God's good reign. Still, the reality of God's good reign is here among us. We just need eyes to see and faith to believe.

There's a mountain called Guye Peak visible at the end of my street. When I want to know the current weather, I walk out onto the road and look north. Sometimes Guye is visible and other times you'd never know he's there because he, and his sister peak named Snoqualmie, are concealed in fog. Some days the soup is so thick you'd never know I live in the mountains. The mist has shrouded reality so thoroughly that it may as well be Saskatchewan (famously flat!). Mountains? Not here. Not today.

Except they are here today. They're real and lasting. It's what's hiding them that's vaporous and passing away. Just wait. Just watch. You'll see.

It's on days like those that I close my eyes and recall the peaks, the wildflowers, the sunshine, the life giving birth to life, the scent of hope and joy riding on the wind. "Yes, the mountains are still there. This fog? It too shall pass."

Our world is foggy and the haze thickens as our news gives us access to more visuals of suffering in a day than someone would see in a lifetime 100 years ago. As the mist thickens, it overwhelms other realities, and we begin to think its what matters most. The buying and selling, climbing and fighting, the aligning with power, or resisting it. Live by the rules of the fog and you'll find tribalism and nationalism, ideological wars and doctrinal wars. Hopefully it all ends up feeling gross and disgusting as we see the fog creating arguments and divisions out of everything from the fast food you buy to your view on masks and the current president.

Don't worry though. The fog will clear. When it does we'll see what Isaiah calls the *"mountain of God."* It's beautiful. People go there to worship and gain justice, reconciliation, and peace along the way. I know people who are ascending that mountain all the time, in spite of the fog. They're feeding the hungry, caring for immigrants and those facing housing challenges. They're fixing marriages and raising hopeful children. They're speaking truth to power and caring for creation.

The mountain of God is there all the time, alive and well. No fog of disinformation, political posturing, consumerist seductions, or denominational bickering can make it go away. Those who are in Christ see it. Those who see it ascend it. Those who ascend it are learning to live the lives for which they are created. Care to join them?

Let's go!

FOREST FAITH is a book for those who understand that their yearning for nature and God are connected. Richard's words of wisdom wrap language around our heart's desire to connect with Christ through deep love of trees and observations of the forest.

RICHARD DAHLSTROM serves as the senior pastor for Bethany Community Church, where he's been the senior pastor for 25 years. He shares his wisdom and experience with faith through authoring three books and working with Torchbearer Ministries, teaching in both North America and Europe.
spiritsoulbody.org

ABBY ODIO is a pastor, lover of the great outdoors and poetry enthusiast. She currently serves at Bethany Community Church as Pastor of Teaching and Formation. Most weekends Abby can be found adventuring around the Pacific Northwest with her husband, Sam, and two young kids.

ABIGAIL PLATTER is a Seattle based Illustrator. She art directs and leads worship at Bethany Community Church, and teaches drawing and painting at Seattle Pacific University. She feels most at home in the woods with a cup of coffee in hand.
abigailplatter.com
@abigailplatter

© Bethany Community Church 2021

Cover Design by Abigail Platter